Girl Power

Dear Kristne,

   Always Believe In Yourself
                +
      Dream Big!
                Love
          Ms Delena

Girl Power

Women on Winning

Jennifer DeSena and Carmine DeSena

Andrews McMeel Publishing

Kansas City

ISBN: 0-7407-1469-4

Library of Congress Catalog Card Number:
00-045352

Book design by
Holly Camerlinck

All photos copyright © AllSport Photography

Danielle Tyler

Oksana Baiul

*I*n the next century, opportunities for the female athlete to participate in sport at all levels and achieve success in the Olympic Games will be equal to those of her male counterpart.

Donna G. Lopiano, Ph.D.
EXECUTIVE DIRECTOR, WOMEN'S SPORTS FOUNDATION (APRIL 2000)

Cynthia Cooper

*T*he success of the Women's National Basketball Association and the greater visibility of female athletes in tennis, soccer, softball, and the Olympics has made it clear that the doors of professional and amateur sports have been blasted open by women eager to share in the passion and glory of playing hard and winning. To accomplish this, you need determination, talent, and respect. In addition, you need to be inspired to be the best athlete you can be. That's what this book is about. It's a collection of reflections, quotes, facts, witticisms, meditations, and advice to inspire all women, from those on high-school playing fields to those in the Olympic Games. Share these messages from women whose love for sports has made them forces to be reckoned with on playing fields, tracks, and courts around the world.

Read their words, hear their voices, learn their lessons— share their strength.

Martina Navratilova

Girl Power

*W*hen I look into a kid's eyes, I look at an opportunity to make a difference, to steer them . . . on the right path to success, on the path to knowing that they can accomplish anything they want.

Cynthia Cooper
WNBA PLAYER, OLYMPIC GOLD AND BRONZE MEDALIST, AND FOUR-TIME WNBA CHAMPIONSHIP MVP

*A*s girls, we don't celebrate enough of our successes. On the soccer field, the basketball court, or even in the classroom, celebrate all your successes, no matter how big or small.

Mia Hamm
SOCCER PLAYER AND OLYMPIC GOLD MEDALIST

*A*lthough we have many positive influences around us, only we can control our own destinies. The only limitations are those you put on yourself.

Lisa Fernandez
SOFTBALL PLAYER AND OLYMPIC GOLD MEDALIST

*W*hen I was a little girl, I had a dream to play basketball. Luckily I had a mom who told me, "You can do whatever you want. It doesn't matter that you're a girl." We're showing girls they can do whatever they want.

Rebecca Lobo
WNBA PLAYER AND OLYMPIC GOLD MEDALIST

*M*y biggest challenge was getting everyone to believe I had a chance.

Tara Lipinski
ICE SKATER AND OLYMPIC GOLD MEDALIST

■ ■ ■ ■ ■

Be bold. If you're going to make an error, make a doozy, and don't be afraid to hit the ball.

Billie Jean King
TENNIS LEGEND

I'm going to beat everyone in sight and that's just what I'm going to do.

Babe Didrikson
COFOUNDER OF THE LPGA TOUR AND OLYMPIC GOLD MEDALIST

*I*f I always believe in myself, regardless of what anyone else feels, and I'm willing to work hard, then I can achieve anything I want.

Gail Devers
SPRINTER AND HURDLER AND OLYMPIC GOLD MEDALIST

*S*occer has given me a place to express myself, fully and openly. To not be shy. To feel. To be crazy. To try things I might not try. To be honest in relationships. To make mistakes and realize they're not life-shattering.

Brandi Chastain
SOCCER PLAYER AND OLYMPIC GOLD MEDALIST

Brandi Chastain

*Y*ou have to live by the rules. You have to play by the rules. You have to win by the rules. Then when you win enough, you can change the rules.

Lynn St. James
PROFESSIONAL RACE CAR DRIVER

*S*ports have taught me how to set goals, achieve dreams, and perform under pressure. I have learned how to be a team player, how to work for something, how to fail and succeed. I think sports are important for kids because they teach those life skills.

Lisa Fernandez
SOFTBALL PLAYER AND OLYMPIC GOLD MEDALIST

*T*here was no one's style or skill to copy, especially for girls, so I made up my own.

Greta Gaines
FIRST WOMEN'S EXTREME SNOWBOARD CHAMPION

*W*hat's the measure we set for ourselves?
It's all relative. It's just a matter of giving
your personal best.

Bonnie Blair
SPEED SKATER AND OLYMPIC GOLD MEDALIST

I'm not looking for
perfection. I'm
looking for the best
in me.

Martina Navratilova
TENNIS PLAYER AND MULTIPLE
GRAND SLAM TOURNAMENT
WINNER

Bonnie Blair

Don't follow in any footprints; make your own prints, because you are the future of tomorrow.

Jackie Joyner-Kersee
TRACK AND FIELD ATHLETE AND
OLYMPIC GOLD MEDALIST

Jackie Joyner-Kersee

I've seen the changes in women's athletics up close in this country. I got the opportunities my older sisters never had.

Dot Richardson
SOFTBALL PLAYER AND
OLYMPIC GOLD MEDALIST

I hope I just show women that it's okay to inhabit your own body. I'm not just a rah-rah feminist. But it's important to me that people see you can be an athlete and be strong—and also be a girl.

Gabrielle Reece
WOMEN'S BEACH VOLLEYBALL WORLD TOUR COMPETITOR

I didn't choose basketball; basketball chose me. I know God gave this gift to me and I've used it to the best of my ability every day. Basketball is my drug—it feeds me and gives me everything I need. I get a high out of passing, shooting, outrunning my opponents, playing defense. Right now my life is surrounded by it. I'm trying to be the best I can be while I'm here, and after this life is over I have to answer to God. We will both know that giving back has been important to me.

Teresa Edwards
WNBA PLAYER AND OLYMPIC GOLD MEDALIST

No matter what
accomplishments
you achieve,
somebody helps you.

Althea Gibson
TENNIS LEGEND

I didn't play for my folks; my passion came from within, not from some external source. I believe that's the reason why I'm still playing after twenty years . . . because I play for me.

Julie Foudy
SOCCER PLAYER AND OLYMPIC GOLD MEDALIST

I knew something was wrong with me. I heard something snap. I kept telling myself not to fall on the vault or the gold would slip away, and all that hard work and effort would fall apart in a few seconds. I just said a little prayer and asked God to help me out. I don't know how I did it. I'll remember this night for the rest of my life.

Kerri Strug
GYMNAST AND OLYMPIC GOLD MEDALIST

Se Ri Pak

I want to be the best. That's my dream.

Se Ri Pak
THE YOUNGEST U.S. WOMEN'S OPEN
GOLF CHAMPION

*O*ne shouldn't be afraid to lose; this is sport. One day you win; another you lose. Of course, everyone wants to be the best. This is normal. This is what sport is about. This is why I love it.

Oksana Baiul
ICE SKATER AND OLYMPIC GOLD MEDALIST

*W*hatever muscles I have are the product of my own hard work—nothing else.

Evelyn Ashford
SPRINTER AND OLYMPIC
GOLD MEDALIST

*T*he sports environment is where girls begin to learn the "rules of the game," rules that they will be faced with no matter where the road of life may take them.

Nancy Lieberman-Cline
WNBA COACH, OLYMPIC SILVER MEDALIST, AND NAISMITH MEMORIAL
BASKETBALL HALL OF FAME INDUCTEE

When anyone tells me I can't do anything, why, I'm just not listening anymore.

Florence Griffith Joyner
SPRINTER AND OLYMPIC GOLD MEDALIST

*N*o matter where you live, what sports you do or watch, how old or young you are, or whether you're a man or a woman, you can make a difference in your life and others' lives by promoting participating in sports and by being an active participant in sports. . . . Be a player in sports and life, not just a spectator.

Lynn St. James
PROFESSIONAL RACE CAR DRIVER

the best things to come out
that we can give American
e heroes, some women they
re—on and off the field. We
ve those when we were
up.

Dani Tyler
SOFTBALL PLAYER AND OLYMPIC GOLD MEDALIST

$\mathcal{W}$hat's happening here is that the young girls of America are getting a message. They're seeing that it's all right to sweat and play hard and get dirty. We don't have to be confined to certain sports. We can excel wherever we want.

Brandi Chastain
SOCCER PLAYER AND OLYMPIC GOLD MEDALIST

$\mathcal{A}$ lot of people think girls cannot do this. I want girls to see that they can.

Fabiola da Silva
AGGRESSIVE IN-LINE SKATER AND THREE-TIME X GAMES CHAMPION

$\mathcal{I}$'m pretty extreme; I expect so much from myself. Why do things halfway?

Michelle Kwan
ICE SKATER AND OLYMPIC SILVER MEDALIST

Michelle Kwan

For all the kids out there who are struggling, and whose peers say they're terrible, I hope I'm an inspiration. If they love it and just keep plugging away at it, something good will come out of it.

Amy Van Dyken
SWIMMER AND OLYMPIC
GOLD MEDALIST

Amy Van Dyken

*E*very day I struggle with my femininity. Boxing is such a boys club—I'm constantly on guard. It's taken a lot of work, but I finally feel that what makes me a woman is what gives me power.

Lucia Rijker
EUROPEAN WIBF BOXING CHAMPION,
1997–98

Serena Williams

I'm tired of losing to people I should beat. Whatever my potential is, I want to reach it now. And if I do, I see Venus as my biggest competition.

Serena Williams
TENNIS PLAYER AND GRAND SLAM TOURNAMENT WINNER

*T*he sky's the limit. I'm still striving, reaching up to the clouds, taking it as far as I can, and just enjoying every single minute along the way.

Rochelle Ballard
NATIONALLY RANKED PREMIERE
BARREL-RIDING SURFER

*A*s simple as it sounds, we all must try to be the best person we can: by making the best choices, by making the most of the talents we've been given, by treating others as we would like to be treated.

Mary Lou Retton
GYMNAST AND OLYMPIC GOLD MEDALIST

I don't have to be enemies with someone to compete with them.

Jackie Joyner-Kersee
TRACK AND FIELD ATHLETE AND OLYMPIC GOLD MEDALIST

Mary Lou Retton

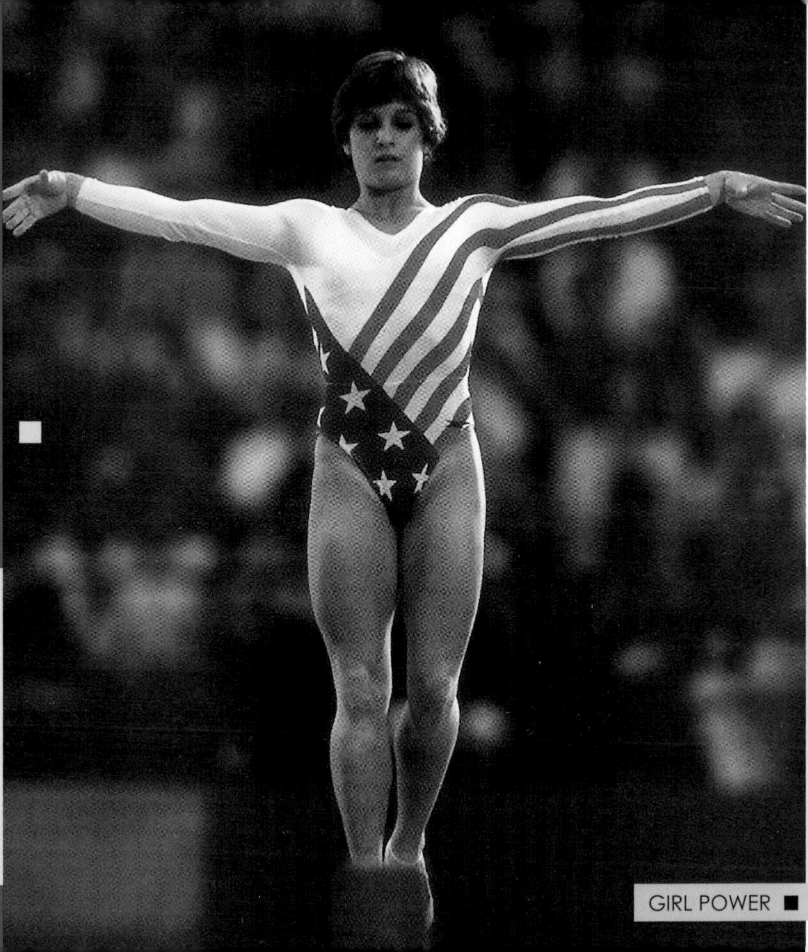

To become the athlete of your dreams, get your mind and body on the same page of your workout.

K. C. Compton
CYCLIST AND WRITER

What I've accomplished, I've accomplished myself. I was never anyone's favorite. I never went to a camp or a clinic or even made one all-American team. Some people have this fairy-tale story. They graduate and they join the tour or the league, and they're successful right away. Mine is a different adventure.

Cynthia Cooper
WNBA PLAYER, OLYMPIC GOLD AND BRONZE MEDALIST, AND FOUR-TIME WNBA CHAMPIONSHIP MVP

*W*henever you meet female athletes there is a bond you share. A lot of them are pioneers, like the women on this team. They understand where we've come from and where we need to go.

Julie Foudy
SOCCER PLAYER AND OLYMPIC
GOLD MEDALIST

*B*reakthroughs are not the result of stubbornness, but of equal parts confidence and will, physical capability and timing, intellectual inquiry and some pure Zenlike letting go. You must do the work and trust the work you've done.

K. C. Compton
CYCLIST AND WRITER

*F*or me, the definition of winning is to reach your potential. I believe all girls as well as boys should be allowed to have this opportunity in sport and life.

Billie Jean King
TENNIS LEGEND

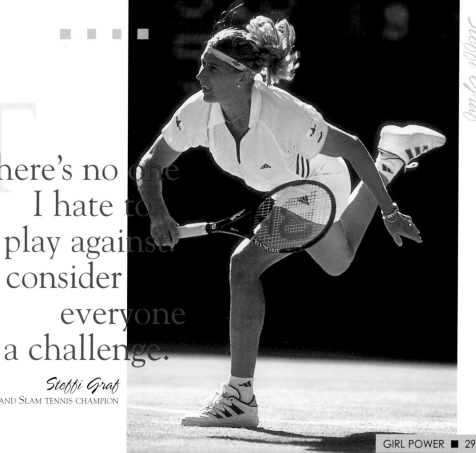

There's no one
I hate to
play against.
I consider
everyone
a challenge.

Steffi Graf
GRAND SLAM TENNIS CHAMPION

Steffi Graf

All of my life I've always had the urge to do things better than anybody else.

Babe Didrikson
COFOUNDER OF THE LPGA TOUR AND
OLYMPIC GOLD MEDALIST

Babe Didrikson

It's the team that's winning all these games, not me. And what we've decided is we have no individual egos, but we do have one big collective one.

Rebecca Lobo
WNBA PLAYER AND OLYMPIC GOLD MEDALIST

Women in sports have to push harder than men for the things they want to achieve. But you can't let society's bias get in the way of what you want.

Shannon Dunn
SNOWBOARDER AND OLYMPIC
BRONZE MEDALIST

I would love to have a daughter, and I would be her coach.

Lucia Rijker
EUROPEAN WIBF BOXING CHAMPION,
1997–98

*Y*ou're playing chess. My body's the board, and my arms, my fingers, my eyes, and my ears are all the pieces.

Juanita Harvey
CHAMPION WRESTLER

A lot of male trainers still think girl jockeys aren't strong enough. But when I was riding you know the body part I used the most? Arms? Legs? No. The brain, that's what. And my brain is as good as any man's.

Patti Barton
WINNING JOCKEY OF OVER 1,200 HORSE RACES

I'm just so much more mature now. I think the biggest thing for me was just mentally believing I should win these tournaments, and that I'm good enough. I've overcome that, and I feel every time I go out there that it's up to me now. A couple of years ago I was petrified. I would never think that.

Lindsay Davenport
TENNIS PLAYER AND GRAND SLAM TOURNAMENT WINNER

*B*ig egos and competitiveness can block teamwork. Luckily, they don't really exist in the WNBA. Neither do women with "attitude." The cooperative spirit among players is not artificial—it's genuine.

Sheryl Swoopes
WNBA PLAYER AND OLYMPIC GOLD MEDALIST

*F*itness doesn't just keep you healthy. It also helps keep you off the streets and away from drugs. If you find a sport you enjoy, it can make a real difference in your life.

Bonnie Blair
SPEED SKATER AND OLYMPIC GOLD MEDALIST

*M*otivation is the key to success in whatever you're doing in life. It comes a lot easier when you're doing something you love and have a passion for. My goal is to have a good time and a hot run. And I'm not afraid of disappointment— it only makes me work harder.

Missy Giove
DOWNHILL MOUNTAIN BIKE CHAMPION,
1996–97

$\mathcal{I}$ am willing to put myself through anything; temporary pain or discomfort means nothing to me as long as I can see that the experience will take me to a new level. I am interested in the unknown, and the only path to the unknown is through barriers, an often painful process.

Diana Nyad
RECORD-BREAKING SWIMMER AND SPORTSCASTER

$\mathcal{T}$ here's competitiveness—but we support each other. It's an incredible thing, how female athletes handle such powerful, conflicting emotions. We're aggressive, but when the race is over we're comforting and caring for each other.

Julie Krone
JOCKEY WITH OVER 3,000 WINS, INCLUDING THE BELMONT STAKES

*H*aving my own Cup boat was a logical progression. If you put on a piece of paper what I'd done sailing, what else was there left for me to do?

Dawn Riley
THE FIRST WOMAN TO MANAGE AN AMERICA'S CUP SAILING TEAM

*N*o, I'm not intimidated by Steffi. I've never been intimidated by anyone, and unless I'm across the net from someone who's ten feet tall and green, I won't be. On the other hand, because of my skills and size, I can intimidate anyone.

Serena Williams
TENNIS PLAYER AND GRAND SLAM TOURNAMENT WINNER

I do feel that women's time on the playing field has come. It's a new day for sports and it's a great day.

Teresa Edwards
WNBA PLAYER AND OLYMPIC GOLD MEDALIST

$\mathcal{J}$ try to combine the qualities of masculine and feminine. If I can be aggressive and competitive, I can do really well.

Missy Giove
DOWNHILL MOUNTAIN BIKE CHAMPION, 1996–97

$\mathcal{S}$uccessful women still push against a constant tide of challenges because they are women. Their struggle isn't personal—it's societal. Everyone wins in an environment where women can be themselves and achieve their potential.

Nancy Hogshead
SWIMMER AND OLYMPIC GOLD MEDALIST

Wilma Rudolph

When I was running, I had the sense of freedom, of running in the wind. . . .When I ran, I felt like a butterfly.

Wilma Rudolph
TRACK AND FIELD ATHLETE AND OLYMPIC
GOLD MEDALIST

*F*ans expect me to win, but I can't let others' expectations inhibit me. Competing should always be for me. That's the only way it can really work.

Gabrielle Reece
WOMEN'S BEACH VOLLEYBALL WORLD TOUR COMPETITOR

*W*omen in sports are no longer pioneering; we're established as a movement and we are growing. I'm proud to be part of that.

Picabo Street
SKIER AND OLYMPIC GOLD MEDALIST

$\mathcal{J}$ust remember that success is relative. You don't have to win a gold medal to be successful. As long as you feel good about yourself, you try as hard as you can, and enjoy what you do, that is success.

Mia Hamm
SOCCER PLAYER AND OLYMPIC GOLD MEDALIST

$\mathcal{J}$ have to develop more technically. I've got a new motivation: I've got to do this. I can't back down. It's like bidding for something at an auction. You want this piece of artwork. Someone bids higher, you don't care. You'll pay more than them to get the painting. That's how I feel now. I'm willing to pay.

Michelle Kwan
ICE SKATER AND OLYMPIC
SILVER MEDALIST

A lot of people have opportunity but no ambition. I think it's more important to have ambition.

Alison Sydor
WINNER OF THREE WORLD MOUNTAIN BIKE
CHAMPIONSHIPS AND OLYMPIC SILVER MEDALIST

$\mathcal{I}$ wonder how many women out there have the potential and capability to do what I've done, but have gone through life without the support system to make it a reality. It makes me cringe to think of parents telling girls they shouldn't play sports because it's not an attractive thing to do and they should do feminine things. Sometimes when women meet me in person they say, "Wow, I thought you'd be really huge and muscular." They think, "Maybe I can do it, maybe it's not an intangible goal." Suddenly that intangible goal becomes realistic.

Julie Foudy
SOCCER PLAYER AND OLYMPIC GOLD MEDALIST

Tomboys are in.

Jackie Joyner-Kersee
TRACK AND FIELD ATHLETE AND OLYMPIC GOLD MEDALIST

*F*or my Olympic long program, I skated to a song called "Rainbow." The rainbow represented my hopes and dreams—everything that I wanted to come true in my life.

Tara Lipinski
ICE SKATER AND OLYMPIC GOLD MEDALIST

$\mathcal{I}$ feel that I'm just a part of what's happening in society. Women are breaking through with much more clout. It's not that we're just breaking around the corner; we're breaking around the corner everywhere with a depth of experience and a depth of confidence. I'm happy to be part of that.

Lynn St. James
PROFESSIONAL RACE CAR DRIVER

$\mathcal{I}$t took a tremendous amount of work and dedication to achieve what I wanted to express on ice, but I loved what I was doing. By creating a unique style, I hope I've opened doors for other skaters to do the same.

Peggy Fleming
ICE SKATER AND OLYMPIC
GOLD MEDALIST

I am the greatest.

Babe Didrikson
COFOUNDER OF THE LPGA TOUR
AND OLYMPIC GOLD MEDALIST

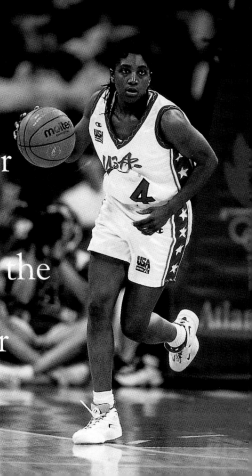

In women's professional sports, there's no room for divas. It's about blood, sweat, and tears. Basking in the glory of greats—that's the glamour of sports.

Teresa Edwards
WNBA PLAYER AND OLYMPIC GOLD MEDALIST

*I*t's irrelevant whether the girls who watch us become professionals. Boys say they want to be like Michael Jordan. Girls should say they want to be like Teresa Edwards.

Jennifer Azzi
WNBA PLAYER AND OLYMPIC GOLD MEDALIST

I've always wanted to equalize things for us. . . . Women can be great athletes. And I think in the next decade women athletes will get what they deserve.

Billie Jean King
TENNIS LEGEND (SEPTEMBER 1973)

$\mathcal{I}$ saw black and white athletes living as one family. The Olympic village was unity. The only place in the world where there was peace. It was home.

Willye White
LONG JUMPER AND OLYMPIC
SILVER MEDALIST

$\mathcal{W}$e were all in a man's sport, and we had all faced the same obstacles and barriers. We grew up having to defend why we play. Our team was loaded with character.

Cammi Granato
HOCKEY TEAM CAPTAIN AND
OLYMPIC GOLD MEDALIST

Gabriela Sabatini

Now when I
lose a match,
I know I lose
on the court—
not in life.

Gabriela Sabatini

I wanted to prove something to myself and others—that anything is possible. You just have to confront adversity head on.

Mary Ellen Clark
DIVER AND OLYMPIC BRONZE MEDALIST

*A*n athlete gains so much knowledge by just participating in a sport. Focus, discipline, hard work, goal setting, and of course the thrill of finally achieving your goals.

Kristi Yamaguchi
ICE SKATER AND OLYMPIC GOLD MEDALIST

Kristi Yamaguchi

*C*hampions keep playing until they get it right.

Billie Jean King
TENNIS LEGEND

Melinda Robinson

Sheryl Swoopes

Lisa Fernandez

$\mathcal{W}$hen I first started coaching softball fifteen years ago, the biggest insult to a woman athlete was to say she threw a ball like a girl. Now I think it's a compliment.

Jennifer DeSena
AUTHOR AND COACH